PREPARING FOR GAME DAY

SOCCER

Breaking Away on the Pitch

PREPARING FOR GAME DAY

BASEBALL & SOFTBALL: SUCCESS ON THE DIAMOND

BASKETBALL: STRATEGY ON THE HARDWOOD

CHEERLEADING: TECHNIQUES FOR PERFORMING

EXTREME SPORTS: POINTERS FOR PUSHING THE LIMITS

FOOTBALL: TOUGHNESS ON THE GRIDIRON

LACROSSE: FACING OFF ON THE FIELD

SOCCER: BREAKING AWAY ON THE PITCH

TRACK & FIELD: CONDITIONING FOR GREATNESS

VOLLEYBALL: APPROACHING THE NET

WRESTLING: CONTENDING ON THE MAT

PREPARING FOR GAME DAY

SOCCER
Breaking Away on the Pitch

Peter Douglas

MASON CREST

Mason Crest
450 Parkway Drive, Suite D
Broomall, Pennsylvania 19008
(866) MCP-BOOK (toll free)

First printing
9 8 7 6 5 4 3 2 1

ISBN (hardback) 978-1-4222-3919-3
ISBN (series) 978-1-4222-3912-4
ISBN (ebook) 978-1-4222-7874-1

Cataloging-in-Publication Data on file with the Library of Congress

QR CODES AND LINKS TO THIRD-PARTY CONTENT

CONTENTS

KEY ICONS TO LOOK FOR:

Words to understand: These words with their easy-to-understand definitions will increase the reader's understanding of the text while building vocabulary skills.

Sidebars: This boxed material within the main text allows readers to build knowledge, gain insights, explore possibilities, and broaden their perspectives by weaving together additional information to provide realistic and holistic perspectives.

Educational Videos: Readers can view videos by scanning our QR codes, providing them with additional educational content to supplement the text. Examples include news coverage, moments in history, speeches, iconic sports moments and much more!

Text-dependent questions: These questions send the reader back to the text for more careful attention to the evidence presented there.

Research projects: Readers are pointed toward areas of further inquiry connected to each chapter. Suggestions are provided for projects that encourage deeper research and analysis.

Series glossary of key terms: This back-of-the book glossary contains terminology used throughout this series. Words found here increase the reader's ability to read and comprehend higher-level books and articles in this field.

WORDS TO UNDERSTAND:

electrolytes: substances (such as sodium or calcium) that are ions in the body regulating the flow of nutrients into and waste products out of cells

neurons: cells that carry messages between the brain and other parts of the body and that are basic units of the nervous system

splay: to move (things, especially your legs, fingers, etc.) out and apart from each other

Chapter 1

GAME DAY

Generally speaking, athletes like structure. They are used to following a set routine, especially on game days. It is a good idea to develop and practice good habits that will have you prepared to perform your best when it is time to kick off.

BE WELL RESTED

The first step in game day preparation happens the night before. Planning to get plenty of sleep is one of the most important steps a soccer player can take to be well prepared to play a match. Ideally, players should sleep about eight solid hours the night before a match, but that should be part of a long-term pattern of healthy sleep habits. Getting four hours of sleep six nights a week and then getting eight the night before playing defeats the purpose. In this scenario, the body will still be tired. Getting regular sleep should be an ongoing practice that includes pre-match nights.

BE WELL FED

When players wake up on game day after a good night's sleep, it is time for breakfast. What and how much to eat at each meal can vary depending on the time of the match. The idea is to give the body the proper fuel to ensure players' legs still have plenty of

"Injury prevention starts with your warm-up. It's always so important to get your muscles ready. It's a combination of running exercises, agility and balance exercises, and it really helps you get the full warm-up before you go out there and play 100 percent with your friends or teammates."

– Alex Morgan, U.S. Olympic and World Cup champion

Starting game day with the proper fuel will help ensure your legs have energy to spare late in the second half.

energy, even in the ninetieth minute. Hungry players will possibly experience light-headedness and fatigue and will find their ability to make quick decisions impaired. Fueling up properly will store glycogen in the body, which provides on-demand energy for hardworking muscles.

Nuts are a good in-game snack to give players an energy boost.

If it is a tournament situation and the game is in the morning, players should have eaten a carbohydrate-rich meal the night before. Options include whole grain pasta dishes or rice and vegetables like squash, beets, and corn. Then the morning meal for a 10 a.m. start should be finished no later than 7 a.m. Try to eat breakfast (or whatever the main meal is before start time) at least three to four hours ahead of kickoff. That breakfast might include whole grain cereal with low-fat milk, a banana, toast with peanut butter, and Greek yogurt.

> 66 Me being a center midfielder I focus on my aerobic base. It's a lot of long-distance running, a lot of 800s. I do a lot of sit-ups and push-ups and strength stuff. 99

– Carli Lloyd, two-time U.S. Olympic gold medalist and World Cup champion

For an evening game, you will need to eat another full meal sometime in the afternoon, no later than three hours before kickoff. This meal should balance carbs and protein. Examples of options include lean meat such as chicken, fish, or turkey (or extra lean beef), with a baked potato, carrots, fruit, and some low-fat milk.

No matter the start time, top up your energy stores with a high-carb snack about an hour before you play. This might be a couple of granola bars, a whole wheat bagel or toast with peanut butter, or even several ounces of whole grain pretzels.

Once the game starts and your body starts to tap into those stored energy reserves, be sure to keep those topped up. Eating an orange at halftime is a good source of energy, as is a snack like nuts.

After the game, it is important to nourish the body to replenish all the energy used during the match and also to help your muscles recover from the intense workout they just endured. Post game is the time for a protein boost. Protein prevents muscle deterioration, actually helping to rebuild muscle tissue. Amino acids are useful in preventing muscle soreness. You will want to eat between ten and twenty grams (0.4–0.7 ounce) of protein after a game. For a morning or afternoon game, this can be accomplished by eating a hearty lunch or dinner soon after playing. Following a night game, a supplement such as a protein shake is a convenient way to quickly get that protein boost.

That post-game meal or protein shake should ideally contain some carbs as well to refill your energy tank. If you came on as a second-half substitute and therefore did not play the full game, aim for eating about one-half gram (0.02 ounce) of carbohydrates for

"Every single sport as a young kid is going to help you because it's going to develop your synchronization of the movement of your body. That's always going to help you if you want to be a footballer or any kind of sportsman."

– Héctor Bellerín, Spanish national team fullback

"When you go to do a free kick, your run-up can't be too straight to the ball because you won't be able to rotate your body and get that movement and whip on the ball."

— Alex Oxalde-Chamberlain, Arsenal winger

every pound (half kilogram) of body weight. If you played the entire game, then that amount should be increased to two-thirds gram per pound. For example, a 150 lb. (68-kilogram) player would want to consume about 100 grams (3.5 ounces) of carbs after playing a full ninety-minute game.

BE WELL HYDRATED

Solid food is only half the equation as far as what soccer players need to consume on game day. Like with sleep and eating habits, serious players will want to maintain good hydration habits at all times as well. Players do not only want to hydrate on game days but should be practicing good hydration habits year round. On game days, however, because you are about to expend a ton of energy and lose a lot of fluids (especially in hot conditions), hydration is crucial. Being hydrated will allow you to be more focused during the match.

A good hydration regimen will see players drinking at least forty-eight ounces (1.4 liters) of water a day, sixty-four ounces (1.9 liters) on practice or training days. On game days, players should drink as usual, but make sure to drink twenty ounces (0.6 liter) about two hours before kickoff. Drink where possible throughout the game, making sure to get another twenty ounces at halftime. The halftime beverage can be a low-calorie sports drink that will help replenish **electrolytes** lost through sweating. Drink another eight

Players lose a lot of fluids on game day, so they need to hydrate properly before they play.

ounces (240 ml) immediately following the game, but keep an eye on your weight loss in hot conditions. More fluid might be required if you notice you have sweat off some weight.

BE LOOSE

Rested and nourished, pro players arrive at the match venue well ahead of kickoff. For high school and college players, the timing may necessarily be a little different, but ideally players will want to start getting their muscles, ligaments, and joints ready to play about seventy-five minutes before kickoff. Stretching is important for all athletes before any activity, whether it be games, practice, or workouts. A routine of light stretching for about twenty-five minutes, focusing primarily on the lower body, will work well for most players. Here is a sample stretching routine for soccer from sports-fitness-advisor.com:

"It's all about putting your teammates in the best possible conditions. Whether it's providing an assist for a goal or playing the penultimate pass, the absolute priority is setting them up as well as you can."

– Dimitri Payet, French national team midfielder

U.S. Navy soccer team players stretch out their quadriceps on the turf.

TWO-LEG HAMSTRING STRETCH

1. With both feet together and legs fully extended, reach forward with both hands toward your toes.

2. Tuck your chin toward your chest to increase the stretch.

3. Keep your toes pointed toward the sky.

HAMSTRING SPLIT STRETCH

1. Bending on one knee, extend the other leg out in front of you.

2. Reach with both hands toward your outstretched foot.

11

3. Keep your toes toward the sky, and tuck your head to increase the stretch. Remember to breathe!

4. Repeat for the opposite side.

LYING QUADRICEPS STRETCH

1. Lying on one side grasp your ankle, and pull your heel toward your buttocks.

2. Keep your back straight and the other leg bent.

3. Do not grab your foot. Grab just above the ankle joint (the bottom of your leg).

4. Keep the thigh in line with your body. To increase the stretch push your hips forward (only a slight movement).

5. Repeat for the opposite side.

CLASSIC QUADRICEPS STRETCH

1. Standing one leg, grab your opposite ankle and pull your heel into your buttocks.

2. Your bent knee should stay parallel with your standing leg rather then being pulled behind.

3. Push your hips out to increase the stretch, and remember not to grab the ankle joint.

4. Repeat for the opposite side.

AC Milan players stretch before a game.

STANDING GROIN STRETCH

1. Stand with your legs wider than shoulder width apart.

2. Shift your weight onto one side as you bend your knee.

3. Reach with one hand toward your outstretched foot.

4. You should feel the stretch right down the inside of your outstretched leg.

5. Repeat for the opposite side.

SITTING GROIN STRETCH

1. Sit with knees bent at ninety degrees.

2. Place the soles of your feet together to **splay** your knees outward.

3. Gently use your hands or elbows to push your knees downward.

LOWER BACK STRETCH

1. Sit with your legs straight out in front of you.

2. Bend the right knee so the sole of your foot is flat on the ground.

3. Turn your upper body toward your right knee, and place your right hand on the floor for support.

4. Place your left forearm on the outside of your right knee, and gently pull your knee toward you.

5. Resist with your knee and left hand to feel the tension in your lower back.

6. Repeat for the opposite side.

STANDING CALF STRETCH

1. Using a wall or bar to support you, place one leg outstretched behind you.

"Don't panic when someone wants to take the ball from you. Try using your hands to create space. And always play forward. Never backward."

– Rafael van der Vaart, two-time Eredivisie champion

"We can't train the ability to focus on the right pass without focusing on concentration, and selective attention, and spatial awareness and other psychomotor and psychosocial skills."

– Tom Bates, performance psychologist, Aston Villa FC

2. Keeping the other leg bent, lean against the wall to apply pressure to your bent leg.

3. Make sure you keep your back heel flat on the ground.

4. Repeat for the opposite side.

CHEST AND BACK STRETCH

1. This stretch can be performed kneeling or standing. Take your shoes off if you kneel.

2. Clasp your hands behind your back, keeping your arms as straight as possible.

3. Try to straighten your arms and raise them.

4. From this position bend forward from the waist, also tucking your head toward your chest.

5. Hold this position for the recommended amount of time.

SHOULDER STRETCH

1. Place one arm outstretched across your chest.

2. Place the hand or forearm of your other arm on your outstretched elbow to apply pressure.

3. Gently pull your outstretched arm closer to your chest, keeping it as straight as possible.

BE WARM

After stretching and getting loose, players should warm up their bodies. Warm, loose muscles are far less likely to get pulled or strained in a game. Soccer warm-ups typically consist of agility drills like short sprints, hops, and quick turns. The focus here is on prepping the body, not on soccer skills. Skills have been worked on in practice and should be well honed by match time. Many coaches do not even use balls for pregame warm ups, although if they do, it should be later after players are already warm. Here are some sample drills for different stages of the warm-up from sport-fitness-advisor.com:

GROUP DRILL #1

This is a good drill to start a warm-up session and makes a change from simply running widths of the pitch.

1. Have the team make a circle about twenty yards (eighteen meters) in diameter (roughly the size of the center circle).

2. Each player should be an arm's width apart from the player to the left and right. Place a cone in the center of the circle.

3. Have the players jog in together to the cone then jog backward to the outer edge of the circle.

4. Vary the runs to the center—high knees, heel flicks, sidestepping, lunge strides, hop on one leg, etc. Keep the intensity light.

The University of Maryland women's team runs a drill.

Watch Manchester United midfielder Andreas Pereira run through a ball control drill.

GROUP DRILL #2

This drill can be used in the middle or toward the end of the soccer warm-up.

1. With a group of six to eight players, split them into two smaller groups of three to four players.

2. Both groups stand in a line facing each other about ten yards (nine meters) apart.

3. The player at the front of group A passes the ball and follows his or her pass to run to the back of group B.

4. The player at the front of group B, who receives the ball, then passes to the next player in group A, and follows his or her pass to run to the back of group A and so on.

5. Each player should focus on a good first touch, an accurate pass, and then an immediate sprint to the back of the opposite group.

6. Gradually close the gap between groups until it is just one yard (three feet) apart. Players literally will have one touch, and they must quickly get into position for the next pass.

7. You can also lengthen the gap to twenty to thirty yards (eighteen to twenty-seven meters) and have the players run with the ball halfway before passing and sprinting to the back of the opposite group.

GROUP DRILL #3

This drill is useful toward the end of the soccer warm-up.

1. Have the team make a circle about twenty yards (eighteen meters) in diameter (roughly the size of the center circle).

2. Four players get into two pairs and stand in the center of the circle.

3. One pair is nominated attackers; the other pair are defenders.

Pregame drills serve primarily to warm players up rather than teach execution.

4. The attacking pair start with the ball. They must keep possession between themselves, while the defending pair try to intercept the ball.

5. The attackers can use the outside players (who should be alert and ready to receive) to pass to.

6. The objective is for the four players in the center to work hard—moving and closing down for ninety seconds. Change to another four players every sixty to ninety seconds.

Players for Premier League team Sunderland execute a drill during warm-ups.

"Once you get in the box, you have time. Most of the time, people want to rush when they are in the box. You have more time than what you think when you get in the box because the defender can't touch you, and basically, you are in a strong position. You have the ball."

– Thierry Henry,
1998 World Cup champion

Even when warm-ups are over, stay active before kickoff. Jog in place, swing your arms—anything to keep the blood flowing to those warm muscles. Use the time before kickoff to get into playing mode mentally. The coach may want to use this time to go over last-minute game plan instructions, but be sure to take some time to gather your own focus on the game to come.

BE IN THE ZONE

The zone—it is that highly desired state of mind where the game comes easily, allowing players to perform at their peak. This is what players should be trying to recapture as they prepare to take the field for a match. Players should focus on remembering back to their best performance, recalling what it felt like to perform at his or her best, recreating in his or her mind the same levels of confidence, skill, and success. Focusing on these positive experiences will help drive thoughts of doubt, fear of failure, worry, and indecision out of your mind, leaving only your best moments. This will activate the **neurons** in your brain associated with physically excelling at given skills. This kind of mental programming helps prepare the body to do what you want it to do and is part of the overall mental preparation soccer players need to perform at a high level.

TEXT-DEPENDENT QUESTIONS:

1. Give some examples of a carbohydrate-rich meal.

2. Approximately how many minutes before kickoff should players start getting their muscles, ligaments, and joints ready to play?

3. Define "the zone."

RESEARCH PROJECT:

Put together a routine to follow for your next game day. Research and get advice on what you should eat and when. Write up a schedule for yourself including sleep, meals, and hydration. Don't forget to include a mental routine to get yourself in the right mind-set to play.

WORDS TO UNDERSTAND:

chafing: to cause soreness or damage by rubbing against something (such as your skin)

porous: having small holes that allow air or liquid to pass through

psychometrics: the technique of mental measurements; the use of quantitative devices for assessing psychological trends

THINK THE GAME

As with any sport, soccer is a lot more fun when everyone can enjoy it safely. Parents, coaches, and players need to make sure that safety guidelines are followed closely. Being safe happens both off the field and on it. Off the field, make sure to get enough rest, be alert, and have a good diet. On the field, players should make sure they are always in control of their movements and are respecting other players. Safety doesn't just happen and isn't just a list of things not to do. Safety consists of being proactive about playing the game responsibly and well. Success in soccer depends on commitment and confidence.

Thinking positive thoughts, like putting the ball in the back of the net, will help boost a player's confidence.

> *You can't go out there and hide. You need to get on the ball and enjoy it, and you don't enjoy it unless you're on the ball. You always want to be looking for it and trying to help the team as much as you can. It's definitely important that you're confident.*

– Dele Alli, Tottenham midfielder

COMMITMENT

Committing to a goal means focusing on working hard at it and not giving up until it is achieved. A possible goal could be to have more endurance or to shoot with more accuracy. Work toward your goal gradually in small steps. Then increase the difficulty of your task, for instance, running farther and farther distances or practicing shots from farther away when working on accuracy. Make sure that you practice consistently. The more often you practice, the greater your results will be.

CONFIDENCE

Believing you have what it takes to succeed is a big part of achieving actual success. If you practice consistently and attain more control over the ball, then you'll experience a high boost in self-confidence. A strong attitude is as valuable as skill.

Think positive, confident thoughts in every situation, such as these:

- No matter how skilled the other team seems, it is only as good as its next game.

- The rival team has the same number of players, who are only human, just like me.

- If I play my absolute best, I will help my team beat even a more experienced team.

- Remember, anything can happen—and anything often does happen.

- The only surefire way to lose is to think about losing. I have the will to win. By keeping confident, I can take advantage of any situation.

Knowing the tactics of the game plan is an important part of mental preparation for soccer.

SIDEBAR

Superstition

Many sports have athletes who, for one reason or another, are deeply superstitious. Soccer is no different. Here are five examples.

1. Portuguese superstar Cristiano Ronaldo is one of the greatest players in the history of the sport, and he attributes much of his success to his . . . hair? Ronaldo will only play games if he has had a haircut that day.

2. During the 1998 World Cup, French defender Laurent Blanc had a unique pregame ritual. He would kiss the top of goalkeeper Fabian Barthez's shaved head moments before kickoff. The French ended up winning the tournament.

3. Leighton Baines of England cannot help himself once he steps onto the field before a match. Despite the fact that there is nothing wrong with his shoelaces, he is compelled to untie them and retie them as soon as he crosses over the touch line.

4. Sometimes a superstition can be so powerful that it affects the game itself. Kolo Toure of the Ivory Coast believes so strongly in being the last man on his team to go onto the field before each half of every match that he once missed the start of the second half waiting for a teammate who was not even playing in the game to come out of the locker room.

5. Spanish midfielder Cesc Fabregas wears a ring that he must kiss exactly four times just before the match begins.

Former Arsenal striker and French international World Cup champion Thierry Henry discusses the game tactics of Barcelona manager Pep Guardiola.

GAME TACTICS

Tactics are the specific plays or schemes coaches devise to support both offensive and defensive strategies. Playing as a team is crucial to soccer; if the best soccer player in the world was playing with an uncooperative team, he or she would not go far. A coach will come into a game with a plan and will instruct the team prior to the game as to what the strategy in the game will be. The coach may want to take advantage of a hole in the rival team's defense, or he or she may have noted a particularly weak offensive player when watching the team's last game. Soccer players need to understand commonly used terminology. The following is a sample of the tactical ideas and terms that a coach will use:

Pressuring the ball is an effective tactic to cause turnovers.

- Pressure: When playing defensively, the defenders should increasingly add more pressure on the ball as it moves to the goal line. A defensive player can mark the opposing team, which means he or she does his or her best to prevent the opponent from passing or continuing toward the net. Applying pressure does not always mean trying to steal the ball. At times herding, which is moving a player toward a direction he or she doesn't want to go in order to steal the ball, can be more effective than an all-out attempt to regain possession. If the offensive player is confronted directly, he or she can easily go around the defensive player. Herding and marking both gradually limit the offensive player's options until he or she must give up the ball.

- Slowing down the game: When your team is winning, your coach may want to slow the pace of the game. This does not mean deliberately wasting time; instead your team should attempt to keep possession of the ball for as long as possible while trying to score again. If your team is winning, the more time your team keeps the ball, the less time the other team has to come back. To keep possession, an effective team will make accurate passes. Also, individual team members must control the ball precisely when they have possession. This combination of good team playing and individual talent helps not only keep the ball but also win games.

SPORTS PSYCHOLOGY

Sports psychology is the study of how sports performance is affected by psychological factors and also the practice of helping athletes overcome those factors to improve performance. Professionals with the Association for Applied Sport Psychology (AASP), for example, aim to employ psychological assessments and **psychometrics** to help through either educational or clinical means.

Educational sports psychologists use methods including imagery, goal setting, and self-talk. Clinical sport psychologists can focus on the influence of the social environment on a player's personality and behavior, the way thoughts influence behavior, or how brain processes affect physical ability.

Soccer teams, especially on the international level, have employed sport psychologists more and more in recent years. While coaches are good

Many sports psychologists teach players relaxation exercises to help them stay calm.

judges of their players' abilities, sport psychologists can also look into the mental factors that go into each player's performance, including motivation levels and alertness. Sports psychologists aid coaches in forming teams with differing psychological approaches to soccer.

Self-hypnosis and relaxation exercises are favored tools of sport psychologists to help players calm down. During mental imagery sessions, players picture themselves performing skills and actions during a game. Self-hypnosis allows players to focus their attention. Other techniques include goal setting, concentration, and self-confidence sessions.

GEAR YOU NEED

All clothing and equipment is regulated. Players are not allowed to use equipment or wear jewelry that is dangerous to other players. The basic required equipment includes a jersey or shirt with sleeves, shorts, shin guards, socks (that must cover the shin guards completely), and proper footwear.

Shoes are by far the most important piece of equipment soccer players use. Many players have a pair for practice and a special pair reserved only for games. A good soccer shoe has the following characteristics:

- completely covers the foot

- has a rigid heel

- has a flexible front to the foot

- has a wide sole

A good pair of soccer shoes is the most important player equipment.

- has good padding on heel and sides

- is made of leather

- fits snugly on the foot

Proper maintenance is important to keep your shoes in top condition. Make sure that you look after them between games.

- When you take them off, untie the laces properly.

- Remove soil or mud by banging the shoes against a wall, and use a brush to get the rest off. Then wipe the shoes with a damp cloth. Never use soap or detergent to clean your soccer shoes—you will damage the leather.

- If they are wet, stuff them with newspaper (to keep them in shape), and allow them to dry. Do not dry them with a hair dryer, or you could crack them.

- When dry, polish and coat them with a waterproof polish or spray.

- If your shoes have screw-in cleats, grease them occasionally to prevent rusting.

- Damaged cleats can cause serious injury—replace broken ones.

- Never over tighten screw-in cleats—you will damage the threads.

- Avoid walking on hard surfaces, such as concrete or stone, when you are wearing cleats.

OTHER GEAR

Players who suffer injuries to the lower leg are most likely not wearing adequate shin guards. The best shin guards have ankle pads that offer both protection and support.

The shin pad fits under soccer socks, which are designed to be snug and keep the pads in place. This fabric holds the pads in a firm grip and allows the feet and legs to breathe and moisture to escape.

In past decades, shorts were snug fitting, but modern soccer shorts should fit loosely for the sake of mobility. If extra support for the thighs is needed, a player could wear spandex shorts or cycling shorts underneath. Soccer shorts and shirts are made of lightweight materials and are **porous**, which allows for sweat to escape and the clothes to stay dry. Some players wear undershirts in cold weather. Any undershirts should be lighter and should not have any seams (to reduce **chafing**). Female soccer participants should also wear a good sports bra and possibly a supportive sports undershirt.

The league you play in will dictate which size soccer ball is used, from the small-sized number three to size five, which is used in professional games. While training, learn with the ball that suits you best.

The playing surface may also play a part in which ball is used. On grass, a leather ball with a waterproof coating is most suitable. On a concrete or other hard outdoor surface, choose a plastic one that is regulation weight. Regulation weight, according to Fédération Internationale de Football Association (FIFA) rules, is no more than sixteen ounces (450 grams) and no less than fourteen ounces (410 grams) at the start of a game. For wooden

Wearing proper shin guards can help protect against lower leg injuries.

or plastic turf surfaces indoors, there are specially made balls that have a covering similar to tennis balls.

GOALKEEPERS

There are specific equipment needs for soccer goalies. Their shoes should preferably have screw-in, long cleats because the mouth of the goal can get very muddy. And even though they do not dribble the ball or get tackled very often, keepers should also wear shin guards.

Goalies can choose to wear long pants, which can be helpful on hard playing surfaces. These provide padding down the sides of the legs, for cushioning dives. On normal playing fields, shorts should be worn. These, too, have padding, and provide protection.

The jersey of each keeper must be a different color than his or her teammates' jerseys or the jerseys of the opposing team. Goalie jerseys should also provide padding, especially down the arms and the sides.

Most goalies prefer to wear gloves. These gloves are specifically designed for soccer goaltending. The gloves should have a rubber covering at the front and should also be well padded with a fastening at the wrist.

Goalies may also choose to wear a hat to keep the sun out of their eyes on bright days.

Goaltenders wear different-colored jerseys and thick, padded gloves.

TEXT-DEPENDENT QUESTIONS:

1. Give three examples of positive, confident thoughts a player should have on game day.

2. What is the study of how sports performance is affected by psychological factors and also the practice of helping athletes to overcome those factors to improve performance?

3. List four key characteristics of a good soccer shoe.

RESEARCH PROJECT:

Do some research on what types of shoes and cleats are best for different field conditions and types, from wet and muddy, to dry and baked, to natural and artificial.

WORDS TO UNDERSTAND:

anaerobic exercise: strengthening muscles by forcing them to work very hard for a brief time while not using oxygen

dispossessing: Taking something (i.e. the ball) away from someone else

equidistant: located at the same distance

Chapter 3

TRAINING FOR SUCCESS

WARM-UP

Warming up is essential before any athletic activity. Cold muscles snap or tear more easily. Warming up means literally exactly that: raising the body temperature by doing light exercise. Start by walking briskly, then transition into a gentle trot, finally sprinting. Try exercises that loosen the joints: shoulder rotations, side bends, torso twists, and knee lifts. Here are some other examples:

Players do groin and hamstring stretches before a game.

SIDE STRADDLE

While sitting with legs spread, hold one ankle with both hands and move your chin toward your knees. While you do this, keep the leg straight, stopping when you feel the pressure in the back of your thigh. Hold this position for five seconds. Repeat this five times and do the same for the other leg. This will help loosen your shoulders and stretch calves and hamstrings.

SEAT STRETCH

Sit with legs together, stretched straight in front of you. Hold each ankle; bring your chin toward the knees, keeping the legs straight. Hold for five seconds and then repeat five times.

QUAD STRETCH

While lying on your back with one leg straight, bend the other leg at a ninety-degree angle, and press your knee to the floor. Hold this position for five seconds, repeating this five times. Alternate with the other leg.

KNEES TO CHEST

Lie on your back, bend your knees, and bring them toward your chest. Hold the position for five seconds, and then repeat five times.

FORWARD LUNGE

Standing with your feet together, step forward with one leg until the thigh is parallel to the floor, keeping your other leg as straight as you can. Lean forward, and hold for five seconds. Repeat this five times. Reverse the position of your legs and repeat.

THIGH STRETCH

Stand with your feet apart. Bend one leg to ninety degrees, and grab the ankle, keeping the other leg straight. Pull back on the ankle until you feel a stretch in your thigh. Hold the position for five seconds; repeat five times. Reverse the position of your legs, and repeat.

HAMSTRING AND CALF STRETCH

While in a standing position, cross your feet. Touch your toes and hold the position for five seconds. Repeat five times. Reverse the position of your feet and repeat.

CALF STRETCH

Lean against a wall with your hands straight out in front of you and one leg bent to ninety degrees. Stretch the other leg as far as is comfortable while keeping your foot on the floor. Press forward, and hold the position for five seconds, repeating five times. Reverse the position of the legs and repeat.

Soccer players help each other stretch on the field.

TRAINING

Training is important for every sport, but soccer players need exceptional fitness if they are going to be able to play at a high level for the duration of a match. No other major sports are played on bigger fields or have as much playing time as soccer. The average soccer player runs between four and seven miles (six to eleven kilometers) per match. One study found that in a match, 24 percent of a player's time is spent walking, 36 percent jogging, 20 percent running, 11 percent sprinting, 7 percent walking backward, and only 2 percent in possession of the ball. Soccer taxes the body at unmatched levels. A player needs to train his or her body to deal with the levels of stress that are involved in soccer.

Check out these ten drills to ramp up your fitness level for playing soccer.

Exercise can be broken into two major categories: aerobic exercise and **anaerobic exercise**. Aerobic exercises consist of getting the heart to beat harder, allowing oxygen to travel through the body more freely. Anaerobic exercise creates muscle mass and does not make the heart or lungs more tired. A soccer player may need different amounts of aerobic exercise depending on his or her position. A midfielder covers more of the field and so needs to concentrate on aerobics more than offensive players who need to work on quickly reacting muscles.

ANAEROBIC EXERCISE

WEIGHT TRAINING

About 90 percent of soccer consists of aerobic activity, but a strong base of anaerobic training makes a big difference in the other 10 percent. A player needs strong muscles to forcefully kick the ball. For soccer players, however, the goal of weight training is not to get bulky, big muscles in the arms or torso. Ideally, weight training will instead make leg muscles strong and fast with outstanding endurance.

> " I think it's really important to maintain the sharpness in your body, the explosiveness and the strength, the power. You always have to find a way to become better.
>
> – Romelu Lukaku, Chelsea striker "

PLYOMETRICS

A soccer player needs to react quickly to fast-changing situations on the field. Plyometric exercises are designed to increase muscle response time and build explosive power. Here is a list of plyometric guidelines:

- Do these activities at the beginning of your training session.

- Even if you are not tired after performing plyometrics, do not continue with other exercises immediately.

- Work out at as fast a speed as possible without losing the quality of what you are doing.

- Do not overdo these exercises; two sessions per week with a full day of rest spaced between the workouts is ideal. Also, if you feel soreness or acute pain, then stop doing plyometric exercises.

To train using bounding, set out ten small cones as obstacles three feet (one meter) apart in a straight line. Then, in a semi-squat position jump as far and high as possible over each obstacle. (Anything of similar size can be used as an obstacle to be jumped over instead of the cones.) Repeat three times.

AEROBIC EXERCISE

Increased endurance is the number one training goal of a soccer player. The more endurance players have, the better they can perform, especially near the end of ninety-minute games. Soccer players who have the benefit of aerobic training will also be able to recover faster from a tiring sprint. The following are a few suggestions for achieving greater aerobic fitness.

- Long-distance jog: Run at half your capacity for two miles (three kilometers) or more. If you do this once every three days, you will greatly benefit your heart rate, circulation, and lungs.

- Medium-distance run: Run close to your full-potential speed for one mile (a half kilometer). This exercise tones leg muscles and also has aerobic benefits.

Soccer is physically demanding and requires a high level of endurance.

SIDEBAR

The Best Players in the World

Who is the best soccer player in the world? The debate since 2008 has raged between fans of Argentina's Lionel Messi and Portugal's Cristiano Ronaldo. Adding fuel to this fire is the fact that these two soccer wizards play for bitter rival Spanish clubs Barcelona and Real Madrid, respectively. Either one player or the other has been named as the world's best player every year since 2008, with five wins for Messi and four for Ronaldo. Here are the top ten performers in the world in the most popular sport on the planet.

1. Lionel Messi of Argentina, Forward

2. Cristiano Ronaldo of Portugal, Forward

3. Luis Suárez of Uruguay, Forward

4. Neymar of Brazil, Forward

5. Gareth Bale of Wales, Forward

6. Manuel Neuer of Germany, Goalkeeper

7. Andrés Iniesta of Spain, Midfielder

8. Sergio Agüero of Argentina, Forward

9. Arjen Robben of Holland, Midfielder

10. Zlatan Ibrahimović of Sweden, Forward

Honorable mention could go to players like Paul Pogba of France or Robert Lewandowski of Poland, among a host of other talented superstars.

SOCCER SKILLS

There are dozens of drills that could help soccer players improve their soccer skills. Here are two examples of skills players work on, one for offense and one for defense.

HEADING THE BALL

In a sport that forbids touching the primary object with your hands, using the parts of your body that can touch the ball well is essential. Heading the ball is the act of striking the ball with your head instead of your foot, most often for balls kicked or thrown high in the air. When attempting to head the ball, watch it at all times, and try to judge where it is going.

- Standard header: Lean your head back, then bring it forward to meet the ball with your forehead. The power of your header depends on how fast you move your head forward.

- Back header: Meet the ball with the rear of the top of your head. Power depends on how quickly you move your head toward the ball.

- Side header: Start with your head somewhere near your shoulder, then bring it up to meet the ball when it is upright.

- Glancing header: Your head should meet the ball and attempt to steer it in another direction.

Controlling the ball with the head is a skill unique to soccer.

Height is an advantage for players when heading the ball, but shorter players can be successful as well. Timing, the ability to jump, and having proper technique to generate sufficient power in the strike are the key components.

TACKLING

The art of **dispossessing** the opposing player with the ball is called tackling. Tackling challenges can be made from a standing position or initiated by sliding at the ball. You must touch the ball before you touch the player; otherwise, it is a foul. Using the bottom of your foot to tackle is also a foul because it could result in serious injury.

- Block tackles: Use your foot to rob a player of the ball by blocking the progress of the ball.

- 50/50 ball: When the ball is **equidistant** from you and your opponent, you obviously want to get there first. If you can, try to make a short pass to one of your teammates; if not, go for a block tackle.

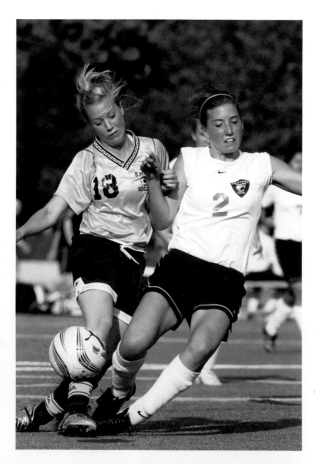

- Interceptions: Taking control of the ball when it is passed or dribbled.

- Barging: It is legal to lean into a player with your shoulder when he or she has the ball.

Full-on body checking is not allowed, but you can couple a shoulder lean with a sliding tackle. Tackling from behind is dangerous and illegal and will result in a free kick for the opposition and probably a caution for you.

This is an example of a barging tackle, a key defensive skill of the sport.

TEXT-DEPENDENT QUESTIONS:

1. The average soccer player runs a range of about how many miles per match?

2. What kind of exercises are designed to increase muscle response time and build explosive power?

3. Define heading the ball.

RESEARCH PROJECT:

Look into what is required to put together an effective off-season training program. What types of non-soccer activities are best to keep players in game shape? How might off-season training vary by position?

WORDS TO UNDERSTAND:

Achilles tendon: the strong tendon joining the muscles in the calf of the leg to the bone of the heel

Contusions: injuries that usually do not break the skin

Ultrasound: a method of producing images of the inside of the body by using a machine that produces sound waves that are too high to be heard

Chapter

TAKING CARE OF THE BODY: INJURIES AND NUTRITION

When a player is hurt, doctors recommend the PRICE treatment for most injuries:

P: Protect—stop training, and avoid any unnecessary activity.
R: Rest—take the weight off of the injured area.
I: Ice—apply an ice pack for around twenty minutes, repeating hourly for four hours.
C: Compression—wrap the injury with a bandage or tape.
E: Elevation—raise the injured part of the body to reduce swelling.

FOOT

Given that they are moving nonstop and frequently get stepped on during games, feet are often injured in soccer. Minor foot injuries can be treated with the PRICE method. More serious injuries like stress fractures require complete rest and can take from six to twelve weeks to heal.

Plantar fasciitis is the inflammation of the ligament connecting the heel to the toes. This causes pain at the base of the heel and is common in athletes who run for extended periods. Stretching the **Achilles tendon** and calf can bring some relief, but rest is the most effective treatment.

ANKLE

Unsurprisingly, sprains are the most common form of ankle injury. The stretching or tearing of ankle ligaments causes a sprain. Symptoms include joint instability, pain, and swelling. An emphasis should be placed on the rest element of the PRICE method; no weight should be placed on the ankle for twenty-four hours or more. Ice should be applied to the swollen ankle.

Applying ice to an injury immediately helps reduce swelling and pain.

Elevating the ankle will reduce swelling. Massage and physical therapy should be used as well as anti-inflammatory medication and **ultrasound** treatments.

A more severe acute injury is a broken or fractured ankle. This injury is characterized by sudden, severe pain and bruising. The broken area will be tender and bruised, and there will be great pain if weight is put on it. Broken ankles require medical attention. They can take up to six weeks to fully heal, but it could take months before a soccer player can safely play again.

At the back of the ankle, the Achilles tendon connects muscle in the lower leg to the heel bone. If the Achilles tendon is strained, it will feel tender and swollen. If the tendon is ruptured, the soccer player will feel the tendon snap and will be unable to raise his or heel or point his or her toes. An athlete with this injury should seek medical attention as soon as possible. Surgery may be required; doctors can treat the injury by putting the leg in a cast. The rupture takes up to ten months to heal, and more time will be needed to get back into shape to play soccer again.

LOWER LEG

Shin splints are caused by overuse or from running on hard surfaces. The most common shin splint symptom is soreness of the shin. The injured athlete should use the PRICE method to reduce pain. Heat treatment should be used on the injured area, and the shin should be taped until swelling stops. Medical treatment is often necessary, and treatments can range from anti-inflammatory medication to massage sessions and physical therapy.

CALF

A calf strain can be treated with the PRICE method. Make sure to keep weight off the injured leg for two days. Anti-inflammatory medication should be used. After the pain and swelling subsides, it is OK to resume light exercise, but be conscious of overextending the body.

KNEE

Runner's knee, or patella femoral pain syndrome, is the most common knee injury. The second most common is Osgood Schlatter disease, characterized by pain and bumps below the kneecap.

Lower body injuries to the feet, ankles, and knee are common in soccer.

Use the PRICE method for damage that can heal within a few days. More severe injuries like ligament tears (characterized by sharp pain and swelling) need medical treatment, and surgery is a likely treatment, followed by three months of rest and then rehabilitation exercises. Ultrasound and physical therapy are both other treatments that may be recommended by a doctor.

Knee ligaments can be damaged, including the medial collateral ligament (MCL) and anterior or posterior cruciate ligament (ACL or PCL), by sharp twists or blows to the knee. Symptoms include instability, swelling, and severe pain, especially when the lower leg is moved. The injured player should use the PRICE method first and ask for medical help. Rehabilitation from major knee damage can take up to a year.

THIGH

Bruises or **contusions** are caused when a muscle is crushed against the bone. Minor contusions vary widely in their severity and can be treated with the PRICE method. Athletes can continue to stretch their quads so long as no pain is caused. Serious contusions involve severe pain and swelling and require immediate medical attention. Doctors can treat major contusions with ultrasounds and surgery. Massage therapy can also help. Recovery time depends on the severity of the contusion, ranging from days to months.

Like with the calf, soccer players often tend to strain the quadriceps, the large muscle in the front of the thigh. Strains occur when muscles tear. The injured athlete should follow the PRICE method for minor strains, but it can take between three and six weeks before the player is able to fully return to playing soccer. A major tear may require surgery and take up to three months to repair. Ultrasound and massage treatment are used.

The hamstrings are the muscles at the back of the thigh, and soccer players commonly pull these muscles when initiating sudden bursts of speed. The pain ranges from minor to serious; the amount of swelling indicates how serious the strain is. The PRICE method should be used for all strains, but severe cases may also require medical attention. Ultrasounds, massages, and physical therapy are all used to treat these injuries. Recovery may take a matter of days or could require up to three months. Wearing spandex shorts under soccer shorts may help prevent future thigh injuries.

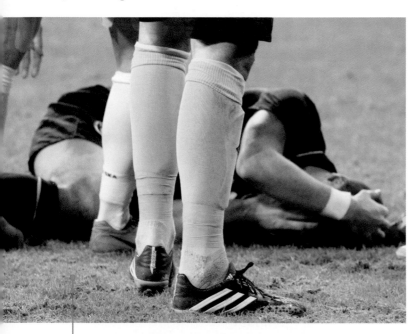

Only football has a higher concussion rate than soccer among youth sports.

A study by the Center for Injury Research and Policy in Columbus, Ohio, found that between 2000 and 2014, close to 3 million soccer players between ages seven and seventeen were treated at hospital emergency rooms. To account for soccer's increasing popularity, the study broke down the data to injuries per 10,000 players and found that the injury rate increased by more than double from 106 per 10,000 in 1990 to 220 per 10,000 in 2013.

Of these injuries, less than two per 10,000 players in 1990 were diagnosed with concussions. In 2013, the rate jumped to almost thirty per 10,000, increasing by about fifteen times. The study acknowledged that increased awareness of concussions and the dangers they present to the health of children were responsible for some of the increase. It also reflects, however, that kids are playing more often. Indoor and winter leagues are now available for kids to play in year-round that were not there twenty-five years ago.

The rate of increase is alarming, but that many concussions occur in soccer in general is no surprise. Data from the Centers for Disease Control and Prevention from 2000 to 2012 shows that soccer ranked only behind football for emergency room visits due to concussions from sports-related injuries for boys, and for girls, soccer was the number one cause.

Clashing heads while battling for high balls is a leading cause of soccer concussions. As a result, the Unites States Soccer Federation has banned heading the ball for kids under ten years old and restricted heading for kids younger than fourteen. Experts stress that proper coaching of heading techniques should be emphasized at a young age to help reduce the number of injuries.

HEAD

Concussions are a serious concern in the sport of soccer, especially among young players. In 2012, only hard contact sports football, hockey, and lacrosse had higher concussion rates in high school age players. A concussion has no outward symptoms other than a feeling of fogginess or

dizziness. Any player who may have suffered from a concussion should be moved away from play and watched closely. If the situation doesn't improve, medical attention should be sought.

For a nose that is bruised or broken in a collision or by the ball, immediate treatment should be used to stop blood flow by plugging the nostrils and applying an ice pack to reduce swelling. If the fracture is serious, the athlete should seek medical attention, especially if the nose is flattened.

Acute pain results from things like collisions with other players during games that cause immediate, localized pain. Chronic pain builds and persists due to overuse of a muscle, joint, or tendon.

OVERUSE INJURIES

Performing the same action over and over again can cause what is known as an overuse or repetitive stress injury. This is not as serious as an acute injury, but any chronic problem may become worse if not cared for early on, so players should seek medical advice and treatment. Overuse injuries have both mental and physical symptoms:

- unusual tiredness or fatigue

- feeling very emotional, particularly depressed, anxious, or stressed

- a lack of appetite

- an inability to sleep at night

- muscle soreness and cramps

- stiff, painful, or unstable joints

- painful tendons

- pain that shows no improvement for more than three days

TYPES OF PAIN

The ability to identify the type of pain being experienced will help soccer players receive better treatment. The two major kinds are similar to the classifications of injury: acute and chronic pain. Acute pain is localized, which means that players experience it in one location. Acute pain has been described as a stabbing or piercing feeling, more intense than chronic pain. Chronic pain feels like a gentler, throbbing ache and usually lasts longer than acute pain. If you are injured, try your best to think of ways to describe your pain.

NUTRITION

Eating right is important for all serious athletes. For soccer players, they need to focus on foods that will help them in their high-endurance sport. Soccer players need to eat a healthy mixture of nutrients to perform at their best. While eating healthy foods is important, an athlete also must decide when to eat, how much to eat, and whether or not dietary supplements are necessary. If you decide to follow a special diet, always consult a nutritionist or doctor.

An active soccer player needs around 2,400 to 3,000 calories to maintain his or her body weight while still providing the fuel needed to remain fit and perform at a high level. All athletes need to eat the correct foods to build muscle mass and burn off excess fat.

In choosing where their calories should come from, players should focus on the proper balance of three major components: carbohydrates, protein, and fats.

An MLS fitness and conditioning coach discusses nutrition for young players.

CARBOHYDRATES

Carbohydrates are foods rich in a chemical called starch, which is what the body breaks down to get energy. Starchy foods include breads and grains, vegetables such as potatoes, cereal, pasta, and rice. There is no one-size-fits-all formula that can exactly dictate what an athlete's carb consumption should be. A general rule is that in season or during times of intense training, athletes should eat about 5 grams (0.2 ounces) of carbs for every pound (0.5 kilogram) of body weight. In the off-season or during periods of lower training levels, it should be about 2 to 3 grams (0.07–0.10 ounces) per pound. The body uses carbs strictly for fuel, so if they are not being burned, they are turned into fat and stored. Therefore it is important to adjust carb intake based on activity level. Athletes should not eat heavily processed carbohydrates such as white sugar and white flour. These simple carbs are quickly broken down into sugars, which the body processes into fats if it does not immediately burn them off. The best carbohydrate choices for an athlete are complex types like pasta and whole grain foods as well as starchy vegetables. A nutritious diet avoids empty calories or those provided by food that lacks other nourishment, like processed sugar and starches.

Complex carbohydrates are a good source of energy for soccer players.

> **After a game . . . that's an important time to get a shake or a protein bar on board. That night as well it's important to carbo load and get carbs back in your system.**
>
> – Jordan Henderson, English national team vice captain

PROTEIN

Unlike carbohydrates, protein is used within the body. Proteins are important chemicals used to perform specific functions inside our body's cells. Our bodies can break down proteins that are found in foods and use them to build new proteins that make up our muscles and bones.

Foods high in protein like meats, eggs, and dairy products help players build and repair muscle.

During periods of intense training and activity, the body needs more protein to repair damage to muscles. Not eating enough protein can cause an athlete to lose muscle mass and negatively affect the ability to perform. The Academy of Nutrition and Dietetics recommends athletes consume about 0.50 to 0.75 grams (0.02–0.03 ounce) of protein for every pound (0.5 kilogram) of body weight. During the season or heavy training, that number should be closer to a full gram (0.04 ounce) per pound. This higher ratio is also true if an athlete is trying to build muscle mass. The best sources of proteins are lean meats and dairy products (such as milk or cheese) as well as eggs and certain types of soy, beans, and nuts.

FATS

Lots of times, we think of fats as bad for us because eating too much of them is unhealthy. However, fat is an important ingredient needed to make our bodies work correctly. They help balance hormone production, support cell growth, and protect our organs, among other functions. Without fats, our bodies cannot absorb certain vitamins as well as they should. Also, our skin and hair need some amount of fat to grow correctly. However, fat should still be eaten in moderation as it is higher in calories than protein or carbs. No more than 70 grams (2.5 ounces) a day is recommended. All fats are not created equal, however. Trans fats and saturated fats found in processed foods are high in bad cholesterol, which clogs arteries and is bad for the heart. The best sources of fat are vegetable oils, olive oil, and nuts.

DIETARY SUPPLEMENTS

Ideally, a balanced diet would provide our bodies with all the nutrients it needs. However, due to many varying factors, eating optimally is not always possible. Dietary supplements are available to fill dietary gaps created by a deficient diet.

In discussing dietary supplements here, this does not include banned performance-enhancing substances. Instead, the focus here is on supplements that contain vitamins, minerals, and other compounds that help the body absorb nutrients or recover more efficiently. When properly used, supplements can improve overall health and performance, but you should always consult a doctor or other expert before using them to augment your diet or training program. Some examples of common supplements include vitamin tablets and protein shakes or powder.

VITAMIN TABLETS

For many reasons, we do not always get the vitamins and nutrients we need. Often, this is because our diets are not as balanced as they should be. Sometimes, it is because the foods that are available to us have been processed in such a way that they lose nutrients. If you know or suspect that a certain key vitamin is underrepresented in what you are eating, in many cases, the necessary vitamins can be obtained from vitamin supplements. These supplements, which are usually taken as a pill, can either contain a balanced mixture of vitamins and nutrients (multivitamins) or contain a single vitamin or mineral that our diet is lacking. The best way to avoid this issue is to work hard to eat right whenever possible.

Supplementing a player's diet with key nutrients may be helpful if he or she is not getting the proper nutrition from food.

Protein shakes are a convenient way to quickly get a good amount of protein in your system.

PROTEIN SUPPLEMENTS

Getting enough protein from the food you eat can be difficult as well. For athletes, eating protein immediately after a workout is recommended (to refuel the body), but most people either don't feel up to or do not have the time to spend cooking or preparing themselves a meal immediately after a workout. That is where protein shakes come in handy. These are protein supplements sold in powder form that look and taste like milkshakes when blended with water but contain no dairy products. Protein shakes deliver a high ratio of protein to carbohydrates and calories. They are not meant to replace meals. Many other necessary nutrients are gained from a balanced diet that cannot be replaced by protein shakes, regardless of how fortified they may be.

STAYING HYDRATED

The body needs water more than it needs any other nutrient. If you are not getting enough water, your performance will suffer in spite of any preparation or balanced diet. Dehydration occurs when your body doesn't have enough water. Symptoms include fatigue, dizziness, and headaches. No athlete can perform at his or her best if not properly hydrated. Proper hydration should be maintained not only at matches but throughout training as well. The body does not store water, so we need to constantly maintain its supply. The American College of Sports Medicine recommends these guidelines for athletes:

- Before Exercise: Drink 16 to 20 ounces (473–591 milliliters) within the two-hour period prior to exercise.

- During Exercise: Drink 4 to 8 ounces (118–237 milliliters) every fifteen to twenty minutes during exercise.

- Post Exercise: Replace 24 ounces (710 milliliters) for every pound (0.5 kilogram) of body weight lost during exercise.

If you are playing in the hot summer sun, remember to adjust your fluid intake accordingly by drinking more. Soccer is physically demanding and takes a lot out of you. Make sure you are prepared to put it back.

Players need to hydrate before, during, and after matches but should also have a daily hydration plan.

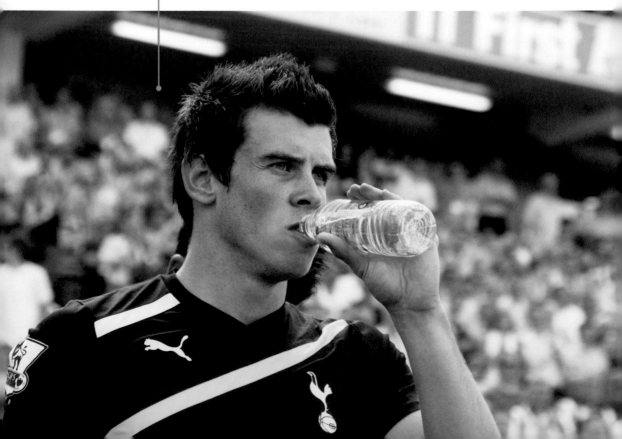

TEXT-DEPENDENT QUESTIONS:

1. What is the most common form of ankle injury for soccer players?

2. The Academy of Nutrition and Dietetics recommends athletes consume about how many grams of protein for every pound of body weight?

3. When does dehydration occur?

RESEARCH PROJECT:

Do some research on dehydration and the effects it can have on the body, including symptoms and effects from low to high levels. How little dehydration does it take before negative effects are seen in soccer players?

WORDS TO UNDERSTAND:

boycott: to join with others in refusing to deal with someone (as a person, organization, or country) as a way of protesting or forcing changes

corruption: dishonest or illegal behavior especially by powerful people

franchise: the right or license granted to an individual or group to market a company's goods or services in a particular territory

Chapter 5

SOCCER: THE WORLD CUP, WOMEN, AND THE WAY FORWARD

ROME, ENGLAND, AND THE WORLD CUP

The sport of soccer is known as "the beautiful game" and is played by millions around the world. The sport's origins, however, are less than beautiful. The game itself is believed to have originated in China more than 4,000 years ago, and over the centuries versions emerged in the ancient societies of Japan, North Africa, Greece, and Rome.

It was the Romans who spread the game to the corners of their vast empire in the first century BC, including to the British Isles. In the centuries that followed, the people of what would become England grew to love the sport passionately. By 1175, there were accounts of a game that evolved from kicking around animal heads, bladders, and stuffed skins. This version of what is now known as association football in the rest of the world (outside of the United States and Canada) did not yet have the rules we now know. In fact, there were few rules at all. Teams included unlimited numbers of players, and violence was commonplace. The resulting

In 1314, King Edward II of England banned the sport of football in his kingdom.

The first formal soccer rules were compiled at Cambridge University in 1848.

broken bones and battered bodies led to a public backlash against the game writers of the time called "beastly fury."

King Edward II banned football throughout his kingdom in 1314. Up in Scotland, King James III also banned the sport there in 1457. These bans, however, were difficult to enforce, especially in rural areas of Britain. Rivalries between villages flourished. Slowly, organization and structure evolved, as did rules. By the beginning of the seventeenth century, the games no longer tended to end in brawls, but instead schools embraced the sport as a chief type of competition with their rivals. The rules were not uniform, however, with the biggest variation being the use of hands. Some regions played a version that allowed players to pick up the ball and run with it, while others forbade handling the ball at all. The first variation would eventually evolve into the sport of rugby, while the second became the modern sport of association football (commonly shortened to simply "football").

The first formal set of rules for the sport was compiled in 1848 by a group from Cambridge University. In 1863, eleven clubs formed the London Football Association (hence the name "association football"). The term "soccer" actually comes from the word "association," which was still slang for the sport when it came to America.

The first soccer match in America played under association rules reportedly took place between teams from Rutgers and Princeton University in 1869. The sport gained popularity at the college level, but attempts to grow it beyond that sputtered. Baseball was the professional sport that had captured the public's imagination and attention at the turn of the century. In 1913, the United States Football Association formed, followed in 1921 by the American Soccer League, a professional league that lasted twelve years before it failed. By this time, tackle football had also come onto the professional sports scene, and Americans had little interest in the sport the rest of the world was embracing.

The Fédération Internationale de Football Association (FIFA) was formed in Paris by founding countries Belgium, Denmark, France, Holland, Spain, Sweden, and Switzerland in 1904. The organization became the governing body for international soccer and remains so to this day. FIFA took over running the Olympic soccer tournament with the 1920 games in Antwerp, Belgium. The sport has been included in all but the very first modern games in 1896, with the exception of the Los Angeles games of 1932. Soccer was left off of the schedule because organizers believed Americans would not come out to watch the matches. When FIFA learned of this decision in 1928, it put together its own tournament, one that has grown into the most popular sporting event on the planet, the World Cup.

This team from Luxembourg competed at the 1920 Olympics in neighboring Belgium, the first time FIFA ran the Olympic tournament.

SIDEBAR

The World Cup vs. the Super Bowl

Americans tend to think of the Super Bowl as the biggest of all sporting events, and that may be true . . . in America. For the rest of the world, however, American football's big game cannot compete with global football's biggest event.

Super Bowl Sunday is like an unofficial holiday in America. Nearly everyone is watching the game or at least are somewhere where the game is being watched. It is annually the most watched show of the year on American television, and it isn't even close. About 112 million Americans watched the New England Patriots win Super Bowl LI in 2017. More than 30 million more watched around the world. So anywhere from 140 to 150 million viewers watched the game. That is impressive but not compared to soccer.

The 2014 World Cup final match featured soccer giants Germany and Argentina. About 26 million Americans tuned in for the match. Around the world, however, viewership was far greater. In Germany alone 34 million watched, with another 20 million watching in the UK. Almost 500 million more watched in the rest of the world. The World Cup tournament had sixty-four total matches. Fifty-seven of them drew more than 100 million viewers or about as many as the Super Bowl does in America.

Soccer is so much more popular than football that even lesser events draw more viewers than the Super Bowl. The UEFA Champions League final, for example, is the club championship of European soccer. Like the Super Bowl, it happens once a year. In 2015, 180 million viewers worldwide tuned in to watch Barcelona beat Juventus, about 20 percent more than watched 2015's Super Bowl XLIX, which was the most watched Super Bowl ever.

Germany has won four World Cups between 1954 and 2014.

The first World Cup was held in Uruguay in 1930 and won by the host nation. Held every four years, Italy won the next two World Cups, but these tournaments were marked by low participation due to **boycotts** by England and the South American teams. World War II then interrupted until 1950, when Germany was banned from entering. It was not until 1954 in Switzerland that a tournament was held without ban or boycott, with countries qualifying from four continents. The Germans won, as they would do three more times to establish their country as a dominant soccer nation.

The nations of Brazil, Argentina, and Italy have also been standout soccer powers over the decades. All have at least five top-two World Cup finishes, with the Brazilians winning five times, the Italians four times, and Argentina twice.

WOMEN, PELÉ, AND AMERICAN SOCCER

Women have also competed in their own World Cup tournament since 1991. Also held every four years, the first tournament had just twelve teams competing and was won by the United States. The Americans also won the seventh edition of the FIFA Women's World Cup in 2015, but that tournament featured twenty-four teams as the women's game has grown around the world.

Unlike their male counterparts, American women have excelled on the world stage. They have won three of the seven World Cups (one more than Germany) as well as four of six Olympic soccer tournaments. The U.S. women were famously led from 1987 to 2004 by Mia Hamm.

Hamm was a fifteen-year-old high school player in Texas when she first made the national team. She was a sophomore at the University of North Carolina when she played for the United States in the first World Cup in 1991, scoring just two goals as a nineteen-year-old. In college, she scored an Atlantic Coast Conference record 103 goals, leading the Tar Heels to four national titles. With the national team, she went on to score 158 goals in 275 games, winning another World Cup and three Olympic medals, including two gold (1996 and 2004). At the time she retired in 2004, 158 goals was an international record for any player, man or woman.

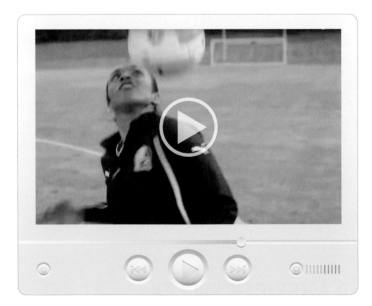

Check out these unbelievable Marta highlights.

Hamm may be the greatest American female soccer player, but the best female player ever is Marta Viera Da Silva, best known simply as Marta. The Brazilian dribbling machine was named FIFA Female World Player of the Year five straight times from 2006 to 2011. Despite her individual brilliance, Marta has yet to will her team to victory in major

Australia takes on Japan at the 2015 Women's World Cup in Edmonton, Canada.

competitions, losing two Olympic finals to the Americans in 2004 and 2008. At the World Cup, her team's best result was runner-up to the Germans in 2007 despite a tournament-leading seven goals from Marta. She is the all-time female record holder for World Cup goals scored.

It should be no surprise that the world's greatest male player also comes from the soccer hotbed of Brazil. Soccer is practically a religion in Brazil, a country that has produced some of the sport's most spectacular players over the decades. None is better than Edson Arantes do Nascimento,

Brazil's Marta has scored more goals in the history of the Women's World Cup than any other player.

known as Pelé. Pelé could never recall exactly how he got his boyhood nickname, but those who watched him play could never forget the brilliance they witnessed. At just sixteen, he played (and scored) in his first professional match for FC Santos, a club team in Brazil. After taking Brazil's Serie A by storm, Pelé became an international superstar the next year at the 1958 World Cup in Sweden. In the semifinal match of the tournament against France, he scored three goals and followed that by scoring two more in the final against the Swedes. With his incredible performance in these two games, the legend of Pelé was born.

> Remember what's important (in crossing) . . . the accuracy. You don't want to lose control of the ball that first touch out. Not too far away from you but not under your feet as well.
>
> – David Beckham, former English national team captain

Near the end of his international career in 1970, Pelé again led Brazil to a World Cup victory, surrounded by what many believe to be the greatest team in the history of the sport. Supported by stars such as Carlos Alberto, Jairzinho, and Rivelleno, Pelé and Brazil went undefeated, outscoring opponents 19–7, including a 4–1 win in the final match against Italy.

After retiring from international play, Pelé continued to play club soccer, ending his career in the United States with the New York Cosmos of the North American Soccer League. The league was six years old when Pelé

Mia Hamm (#9 in white) played her last World Cup for the United States in 2003, when the Americans finished third. Considered to be America's best female player ever, Hamm won World Cups in both 1991 and 1999.

When English megastar David Beckham joined the MLS in 2007, it gave the fledgling league an instant boost in credibility.

Argentina's Lionel Messi has been named best player in the world five times while playing for Barcelona in Spain's La Liga.

arrived, helping to triple attendance at Cosmos games. By 1980, however, Pelé was gone, and interest in the league fell off. What had been the most successful attempt at professional soccer in the United States to date folded in 1984 after fifteen years.

Just four years later, the United States won the bid to host the 1994 World Cup. A condition of the bid, however, was that the host country had to have a pro league. Therefore Major League Soccer (MLS) was formed in 1993. The league began actual play in 1996 and after more than twenty seasons is the most successful U.S. pro soccer league. After initial early struggles and financial losses, things turned around for the league in 2002 after a strong showing by the U.S. team in the World Cup that year. The league received another boost when English superstar David Beckham signed with the Los Angeles Galaxy in 2007. Despite being on the tail end of his career, the signing still brought the league much needed added credibility. In 2016, the league set a high for average attendance at 21,692, up 57 percent from a low of slightly more than 13,000 in 2000.

EUROPE, THE SUPERSTARS, AND THE FUTURE

To say that Beckham was a superstar might actually be understating his status somewhat. He was an international sports icon at the peak of his career, recognized around the world by millions who did not identify themselves as soccer fans. Beckham retired in 2013 after a storied career on the wing with ten league titles. On the downside of his career, his place as one of the world's best players was taken by a pair of dynamic forwards.

Either Portugal's Cristiano Ronaldo or Argentina's Lionel Messi has been chosen as FIFA's best player in the world every year since 2008. Messi has won five times and Ronaldo four. Messi was runner-up to Ronaldo on all four occasions. Ronaldo has also been runner-up to Messi four times. To make their rivalry even more intense, both men have played for Spanish powerhouse clubs since 2009, when Ronaldo moved from Manchester United to Real Madrid for a staggering $128 million. Messi was already at Barcelona, the other top club in Spain's top league, La Liga.

The two teams dominate Spain's La Liga, one of the top club leagues in the world. In 2016, Forbes ranked Real Madrid and Barcelona as the second and third most valuable sports franchises on the planet, at $3.75 and $3.55 billion, respectively, more than the New York Yankees ($3.4 billion) or New England Patriots ($3.2 billion). The Dallas Cowboys, at $4 billion, took over the top spot from Real, which was the most valuable cub from 2013 to 2015. Ronaldo makes about $34 million each season. Messi is paid nearly $43 million. Since Messi arrived in 2004, either Barcelona or Real Madrid has won the league title in every season but one. The two clubs attract the best players in the world, with Luis Suarez and Neymar alongside Messi at Barcelona and Gareth Bale and Luka Modric at Real.

Outside of Spain, none of the other La Liga clubs has the prestige of the big two. The club league in world soccer with the most prestige is England's Premier League. On average, Premier League players earn about $3 million each season, compared to just $1.5 million in La Liga. The top Premiership Clubs include Manchester United, Arsenal, Manchester City, Chelsea, and

Liverpool. The three highest-paid players in the league wear the red of Manchester United, which boasts 350 million worldwide supporters. Paul Pogba is paid about $19 million a season to patrol the midfield for United. Teammates Wayne Rooney and Zlatan Ibrahimovic are not far behind. Other Premier league stars include Sergio Agüero and Yaya Toure of Man City and Eden Hazard of Chelsea. England also has three other tiers of professional soccer that are heavily followed and supported in the soccer-mad country.

Other relevant leagues across Europe include Germany's Bundesliga, where Bayern Munich is the dominant club, boasting stars such as Arjen Robben and Manuel Neuer. In Italy, the top-flight Serie A is making a comeback after years of decline, with clubs such as thirty-two-time champion Juventus attracting top-end players like Gonzalo Higuain and Gianluigi Buffon. In Portugal, the story begins and ends with rival Primeira Liga clubs FC Porto and SL Benfica. Since 1980, one or the other has won the league title in all but four seasons. Powerhouse Paris Saint-Germain and stars Thiago Silva and Ángel Di María dominate France's Ligue 1.

The English Premier League's Manchester United is one of the top soccer clubs in the world.

Argentina's Ángel Di María plays his club soccer in France for Paris Saint-Germain.

Outside of Europe, there is quality soccer in South American soccer hotbeds Argentina (Primera Division) and Brazil (Serie A). Buenos Aires-based River Plate and Boca Juniors are the top Argentine clubs. In Brazil, it is Corinthians and Flamengo.

The domination of the sport by European and South American countries is a concern for FIFA officials. FIFA's position is that the sport should expand to better include nations from Asia, Africa, and the Caribbean. Currently, thirty-two teams qualify for the final World Cup tournament every four years. In October of 2016, FIFA president Gianni Infantino announced, "The 2026 FIFA World Cup may have an expanded 40- or 48-team competition format, pending further analysis of different options by the FIFA administration." Infantino feels this will help increase soccer's popularity, which is quite a goal for something that is already the world's most popular sport.

In a **corruption** scandal in 2015 top FIFA officials were accused of taking bribes and trading votes to influence bid selections. In response to the bad publicity these events cast on the organization, in May of 2016 FIFA announced they would revamp the bid process with a new four-phased approach:

1. Strategy and Consultation—FIFA will review the eligibility of interested member nations on human rights, environmental protection, and technical requirements

2. Bid Preparation—formal bids are submitted from eligible nations

3. Bid Evaluation

4. Decision

However FIFA decides to proceed in the future, there is little doubt that stadiums will continue to be filled. It seems no amount of turmoil off the pitch can deter fans from their love of the players and the beautiful game they play on the pitch.

TEXT-DEPENDENT QUESTIONS:

1. When was FIFA formed?

2. In what year did women begin competing in their own World Cup tournament?

3. Name the soccer icon who retired in 2013 after a storied career on the wing with ten league titles.

RESEARCH PROJECT:

Americans prefer their sports to have lots of scoring, which soccer does not feature. Do some research, and come up with three ways you think would increase the appeal of the beautiful game for American sports fans. Make sure you include the rationale behind your theory.

SERIES GLOSSARY OF KEY TERMS

Acute Injury: usually the result of a specific impact or traumatic event that occurs in one specific area of the body, such as a muscle, bone, or joint.

Calories: units of heat used to indicate the amount of energy that foods will produce in the human body.

Carbohydrates: substances found in certain foods (such as bread, rice, and potatoes) that provide the body with heat and energy and are made of carbon, hydrogen, and oxygen.

Cardiovascular: of or relating to the heart and blood vessels.

Concussion: a stunning, damaging, or shattering effect from a hard blow—especially a jarring injury of the brain resulting in a disturbance of cerebral function.

Confidence: faith in oneself and one's abilities without any suggestion of conceit or arrogance.

Cooldown: easy exercise, done after more intense activity, to allow the body to gradually transition to a resting or near-resting state.

Dietary Supplements: products taken orally that contain one or more ingredient (such as vitamins or amino acids) that are intended to supplement one's diet and are not considered food.

Dynamic: having active strength of body or mind.

Electrolytes: substances (such as sodium or calcium) that are ions in the body regulating the flow of nutrients into and waste products out of cells.

Flexible: applies to something that can be readily bent, twisted, or folded without any sign of injury.

Hamstrings: any of three muscles at the back of the thigh that function to flex and rotate the leg and extend the thigh.

Hydration: to supply with ample fluid or moisture.

Imagery: mental images, the products of imagination.

Mind-Set: a mental attitude or inclination.

Overuse Injury: an injury that is most likely to occur to the ankles, knees, hands, and wrists, due to the excessive use of these body parts during exercise and athletics.

Plyometrics: also known as "jump training" or "plyos," exercises in which muscles exert maximum force in short intervals of time, with the goal of increasing power (speed and strength).

Positive Mental Attitude (PMA): the philosophy that having an optimistic disposition in every situation in one's life attracts positive changes and increases achievement.

Protein: a nutrient found in food (as in meat, milk, eggs, and beans) that is made up of many amino acids joined together, is a necessary part of the diet, and is essential for normal cell structure and function.

Quadriceps: the greater extensor muscle of the front of the thigh that is divided into four parts.

Recovery: the act or process of becoming healthy after an illness or injury.

Resistance: relating to exercise, involving pushing against a source of resistance (such as a weight) to increase strength. Strength training, or resistance exercises, are those that build muscle. They create stronger and larger muscles by producing more and tougher muscle fibers to cope with the increasing weight demands.

Strategy: a careful plan or method.

Stretching: to extend one's body or limbs from a cramped, stooping, or relaxed position.

Tactics: actions or methods that are planned and used to achieve a particular goal.

Tendon: a tough piece of tissue in the body that connects a muscle to a bone.

Training: the process by which an athlete prepares for competition by exercising, practicing, and so on.

Warm-Up: exercise or practice especially before a game or contest— broadly, to get ready.

Workout: a practice or exercise to test or improve one's fitness for athletic competition, ability, or performance.

FURTHER READING:

Luke, Andrew. *Soccer (Inside the World of Sports).* Broomall, PA: Mason Crest, 2017.

Burshtein, Karen. *Lionel Messi: Soccer's Top Scorer (Living Legends of Sports).* New York: Rosen Education Service, 2015.

Teixeira, Thiago Jorge. *Ronaldo (Superstars of Soccer: Brazil).* Broomall, PA: Mason Crest, 2013.

INTERNET RESOURCES:

Fédération Internationale de Football Association: ***http://www.fifa.com***

Stop Sports Injuries: ***http://www.stopsportsinjuries.org/STOP/Prevent_ Injuries/Soccer_Injury_Prevention.aspx***

Major League Soccer: ***http://www.mlssoccer.com/***

FDA, Dietary Supplements: ***http://www.fda.gov/Food/DietarySupplements/ default.htm***

VIDEO CREDITS:

Watch Manchester United midfielder Andreas Pereira run through a ball control drill: ***http://x-qr.net/1DCa***

Former Arsenal striker and French international World Cup champion Thierry Henry discusses the game tactics of Barcelona manager Pep Guardiola: ***http://x-qr.net/1E7D***

Check out these ten drills to ramp up your fitness level for playing soccer: ***http://x-qr.net/1CuH***

An MLS fitness and conditioning coach discusses nutrition for young players: ***http://x-qr.net/1GFe***

Check out these unbelievable Marta highlights: ***http://x-qr.net/1GhY***

PICTURE CREDITS

QR CODES AND LINKS TO THIRD-PARTY CONTENT

INDEX

In this index, page numbers in ***bold italics*** font indicate photos or videos.

ABOUT THE AUTHOR

Peter Douglas is a former journalist, reporting on both sports and general news for many years at television stations in various locations across the US affiliated with NBC, CBS and Fox. Prior to his journalism career he worked with the Boston Red Sox Major League baseball team. An avid writer and sports enthusiast, he has authored 16 additional books on sports topics. In his downtime Peter enjoys family time with his wife and two young children and attending hockey and baseball games in his home city.